JOHN CORIGLIANO

ADAGIO
from GAZEBO DANCES

arranged for solo piano by Dolores Fredrickson

duration: ca. 4 minutes

ED-3898

G. SCHIRMER, *Inc.*

DISTRIBUTED BY
HAL•LEONARD®
7777 W. BLUEMOUND RD. P.O. BOX 13819 MILWAUKEE, WI 53213

for Sheldon Shkolnik

ADAGIO
from *Gazebo Dances*

John Corigliano
arranged by Dolores Fredrickson

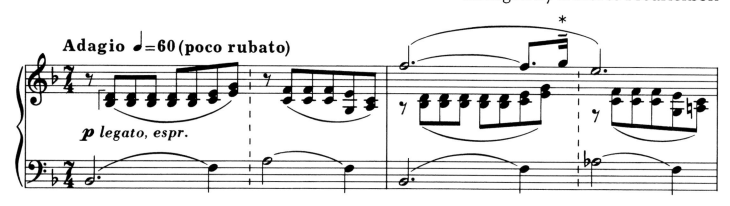

* Always make a slight *ritard.* on the sixteenth note and return to tempo on the next beat.